Make a Instragram Business

How to Make Money With Instragram

By

CLYDEX

Copyright © 2017

digitalexplorerx.com

INTRODUCTION:

Welcome to the **l**atest and **m**ost effective Instagram **M**arketing **S**pecial **F**ree **R**eport, designed to take you by the hand and walk you through the process of Getting the most out of Instagram on behalf of your business. I'm so excited to have you here, and I know this will be very helpful for you.

This excellent and exclusive Special Free Report will take you by the hand and show you step-by-step, topic by topic, and tool by tool what you really need to know in order to dominate Instagram the easiest way possible, using the most effective tools and in the shortest time ever.

This is exactly what you are going to learn from this Special Free Report:

In **Chapter 1** you will learn what Instagram is all about; we will give you the easiest definition for it, as well as how it is generally used for businesses.

In **Chapter 2** you will learn why businesses should definitely use Instagram, as it has such a powerful social marketing reach to help you take the productivity of your business to any level you want.

You will learn about some amazing benefits Instagram can bring to any business, and we will even show you up to 10 fantastic facts that will open your eyes to the immense social marketing power it possesses nowadays.

In **Chapter 3** you will learn how businesses are actually using Instagram so you will know what type of businesses have decided to use it in their marketing efforts and how you can get it done too.

TABLE OF CONTENTS

Introduction: 2
Table of Contents 4
Disclaimer: 5
Chapter I: What is Instagram all about? 7
Chapter II: Why Businesses should definitely use Instagram? 11
Chapter III: How are Businesses actually using Instagram? 16
Chapter IV: How to use Instagram the Right Way - Step by Step 20
Chapter V: The Top 10 Instagram Marketing Power Tools 21
Chapter VI: The Hottest 10 Instagram Marketing Tips 24
Chapter VII: Shocking Instagram Businesses' Case Studies 26
Chapter VIII: Instagram Marketing Dos and Don'ts .. 29
Conclusion: 35
About The Author 36

Disclaimer:

This work may not be copied, sold, used as content in any manner or your name put on it until you buy sufficient rights to sell it or distribute it as your own from us and the authorized reseller/distributer.

Every effort has been made to be accurate in this publication. The publisher does not assume any responsibility for errors, omissions or contrary interpretation. We do our best to provide the best information on the subject, but just reading it does not guarantee success. You.

This publication is not intended for use as a source of any legal, medical or accounting advice. The information contained in this guide may be subject to laws in the United States and other jurisdictions. We suggest carefully reading the necessary terms of the services/products used before applying it to any activity which is, or may be, regulated. We do not assume any responsibility for what you choose to do with this information. Use your own judgment. Any perceived slight of specific people or organizations, and any resemblance to characters living, dead or otherwise, real or fictitious, is purely unintentional.

Some examples of past results are used in this publication; they are intended to be for example purposes only and do not guarantee you will get the same results. Your results may differ from ours. Your results from the use of this information will depend on you, your skills and effort, and other different unpredictable factors. It is important for you to clearly understand that all marketing activities carry the possibility of loss of investment for testing purposes. Use this information wisely and at your own risk.

Chapter I: What is Instagram all about?

Definition:

Instagram is an online mobile photo-sharing, video sharing and social networking service that enables you to take pictures and videos and share them on a variety of social networking platforms, such as Facebook, Twitter, Tumblr and Flickr.

(Source) Instagram was launched in October 2010 and was acquired by Facebook in April 2012. Instagram is mainly a mobile platform, and it is so important for your business because people are increasingly accessing the internet via their mobile devices. Instagram users can view their newsfeed and browse other users' profiles through the website, Instagram.com. This application is currently available only for iOS and Android Phones, and it is freely available in the Apple app store and the Google Play store.

Instagram allows you to capture a moment or choose an image or video and edit it to transform its look and feel. You can then post the images with your smartphone and post your pictures on Instagram for a particular user or all to see. You can capture a series of pictures with your mobile device and share with your friends.

In today's world, marketing is all about sharing the things that are happening right now. Instagram is one of the world's most popular social network apps and a great way to share your photos online. You can see less content-heavy The images with Instagram appear in a square shape rather than 16:9 aspect ratio. The squaring photo format gives a vintage look to your images. Instagram also offers you video sharing options with an available video length of up to 15 seconds.

Instagram is mainly used by people who want to become more social, and it is also widely used by businesses to promote their products and services while connecting with followers. Instagram provides more potential than instant photo sharing, as it allows pictures to generate customers for you and increase your brand reputation.

You can create an Instagram newsfeed with helpful information to boost your followers, engage them with your brand, and generate new content that will drive more customers to you. accounts and more pictures

captured and shared in your daily life.

Many brands are using Instagram as a marketing platform to increase their social engagement with Facebook, Twitter, Google+, LinkedIn, Foursquare, Pinterest and other social media platforms. It is among top 10 most popular smartphone apps, and it can provide a huge asset for your visual content,

which drives social media like none other component.
☐ How Instagram is generally used?

Instagram is mostly used by individuals to share images and movies. However, like the other social sharing sites, it also has business potential. MTV, Foo Fighters, Starbucks and so many other businesses are able to promote themselves and their brands.

You can include virtual tours and behind the scene views for your new product and services, such as how-to videos, company tours, images of your products, and more. No matter what your industry may be, Instagram provides you with the potential to connect with thousand and millions of customers across the globe.

Instagram encourages your customers to connect with you on a more personal level as compared to other internet marketing strategies. You can provide behind the scene video and an image of your product demonstration to make your customers feel like they are also the part of your whole development process.

You can write descriptions and use hashtags to support your video and images.

However, when with Instagram, the real heroes of your online marketing strategies are images and video.

Instagram is arguably the leader in visual representation. But the chances of succeed depend on how you utilize Instagram to increase your engagement and awareness about your brand. Using Instagram, your business model will focus on user experience; that means you can upload more pictures and will get less complaints.

If you have Instagram, that means you have the elegant user interface with which you can communicate using multiple social media channels, and its quality will make you feel like you are working with professionals.

You have to understand the Instagram so that you can build close relationships with your audiences, represent your brand beyond the products you sell, and create the visual strategies that your brand needs.

Chapter II: Why Businesses should definitely use Instagram?

The popularity of Instagram is growing year by year, and its number of active users is increasing day by day. As you know, Instagram is a social media website and a great tool for online marketing strategies.

The uniqueness of Instagram is that it focuses on images, videos and sense of closeness images and videos provide. This makes them a great tool to use for visual marketing. You can instantly post images with your mobile device and share them with your followers to promote your products and services.

You can use Instagram with supportive tools to boost your marketing efforts. If you are offering great products, you can brand your business by showing them your audience in the way you want. But this also requires constant effort and a strategy plan in order to market. You need to find the niche audience before you execute your online marketing strategy with Instagram.

Amazing Benefits

Easy-to-Use: Instagram allows you to create awesome images that you can also use on other social platforms. Facebook, Twitter, Flickr, Tumblr and other social media platform are optimized for images; that's how images are displayed on these platforms, so you can directly share from Instagram.

Instagram is mobile: Instagram merges two great forces that are essential in social marketing strategies: mobile and photo sharing. This can give unique value to your brand.

Visual storytelling: Instagram has more artistic value than other social media platforms. You can use a brand moment that will be more impactful than text.

With Instagram, you can communicate visually with your audience, followers and fans. Here are few ways that Instagram will benefit your business:

Build trust: Personal images humanize your brand and allow you to be more reachable. Instagram allows you to put a face to your brand, and this will help to build consumers' confidence in your business.

It also provides you with a way to build a positive online user experiences and generate leads for repeat customers. Instagram is a great way to share your business experience in an informal and casual way. You can also include behind the scenes and employee images to give a personal touch to your business.

Drive more traffic: Yes, you can drive more traffic to your business with Instagram. When you upload an image to Instagram, be sure that you list your website in your profile and that you add your website URL in description. You can use hashtags, calls to action in post comments, and share your content on other social media platforms to generate more traffic to your website. You can also include amazing content that will encourage your audience to visit your website.

Free exposure: With other social media platforms like Facebook and LinkedIn, you have advertisement buying options according to your goals. But with Instagram you do not have to buy anything. Instagram is completely free, and it will help you to create a great online presence; it may require a lot of time and effort, but it doesn't cost a cent.

Visual marketing: Instagram's simple design allows delectable visuals that include images and videos. You have heard the phrase "A picture is worth a thousand words". So being a marketer, you should take advantage of pictures.

Just be sure to be amazingly creative with your images.

If you see good results with visual marketing on other platforms, then think of the capabilities of Instagram, which is dedicated to visual marketing.

User engagement: Now Instagram has 200 million active users every month -that means a huge traffic. By providing useful and interesting content on Instagram, you can earn higher levels of engagements with your customers.

Studies show that Instagram delivered 58 times more engagement per follower than Facebook, and 120 times more engagement per follower than Twitter.

Get personal: Instagram gives you a chance to show your customers who you are and what you do. With this you can make your business more personable, which leaves a long lasting impression on your followers and customers.

Emotional connection with your customers encourages them to take the desired action, and using emotions in your post can increase your engagement. You can show them behind the scenes stories, video and photo of a meeting, staff posts and birthdays in store, etc. to become more personal.

Build Network: Instagram is also a social marketing platform in addition to an image platform, so use its network. It will help you to meet new audiences and build relationships. In return, you will gain followers, new audiences and potential customers. The value of your customers basically depends on connection. If your connections with your audience are deep and structured then you can monetize your connection with ad-networks like Facebook.

Increase conversions: You can run contests and online marketing campaigns on Instagram. This will increase your followers and engagement with your audience. You need to set a custom reply on each and every campaign entry.

You can add a links, sign up forms, and terms and conditions to your contest in the comments. You need to manually write the links because copy-paste doesn't work with Instagram. This will help you to increase your conversions and lead generation.

Going viral: Instagram also provides you the opportunity to go viral with your images and videos. You can take some time to capture images in a creative way.

Instagram's popular pages show current moments and images, and these visuals are visible to all users of Instagram. You can share incredibly creative and cute images to generate more leads with the potential that it will boost your sales and customer relationships.

Chapter III: How are Businesses actually using Instagram?

Instagram is a great way to reach your new audience with a visual story.

Instagram allows you to enhance your images with filters. Instagram has seen remarkable growth with 200 million active users, and businesses are utilizing Instagram for advertising and branding by building mutual understanding and connection with their customers.

You can use the sharing features of Instagram with specific hashtags to engage your potential customers who have an interest in you. Small businesses and brands are recognizing that Instagram is the perfect platform to create brand recognition and promote services. It also combines the power of images and mobile, which are the powerful sources of social marketing.

Instagram instantly puts a face to your brand; have a look some great businesses that use Instagram to generate their desired results.

Ford Fiesta:

The Ford Fiesta is a supermini car manufactured by the Ford Motor Company since 1976, now in its seventh generation.

The Ford Fiesta has manufactured its cars in

Europe, Brazil, Argentina, Mexico, Venezuela, China, India, Taiwan, Thailand and

South Africa and sold over 16 million units since 1976.

Ford Fiesta used Instagram to run a campaign across Europe that was based on Fiesta's features and was hosted on Facebook fan pages. Ford Fiesta encouraged its audience every week to submit their #Fiestagram tagged pictures.

More than 16,000 images were submitted by people during 6 week campaign.

Facebook fan pages gained more than 1 million new fans. The best pictures were shown live in online galleries and on billboards. The best photo won a brand new Ford Fiesta as prize. This campaign became successful by demographic targeting in the Instagram community.

Burberry:

Burberry Group public company is a British luxury fashion house that deals in fashion accessories, fragrances, sunglasses and cosmetics. This company was founded in 1856 in England by Thomas Burberry, who first designed the trench coat. Burberry has 1,957,637 followers on its Instagram profile.

British Fashion House Burberry wanted to launch its next fragrance with Instagram, as it has already known about Instagram's importance for fashion brands. Burberry gave faces to their two fragrances - British models Kate Moss and Cara Delevingne.

To make this campaign successful, Burberry used candid moments, behind the scenes, and interactive moments of the two ladies which are not often seen in magazines. One image of Kate Moss and Cara Delevingne was liked approximately 35.2K times.

Free People:

Free People is an American bohemian-based apparel and lifestyle retail company. Free People sells women's clothing, shoes, music, art and other accessories. 1,501,972 followers are following free people.

Free people used Instagram as a central feature of their website. It used Instagram applications to encourage their customers to post their pictures on Free People fashion with specific hashtags. Some of the photos were added to the Free People official website.

This campaign allowed customers to see how the products look in real life.

Customers can like, comment on, and create a conversation about the looks that Free People's fans created.

Chapter IV: How to use Instagram the Right Way - Step by Step

Here are the 7 vital steps you will need to follow in order to get the most out of Instagram for your business over the web:

Step 1: Downloading the Instagram Mobile App

Step 2: Creating your Instagram Account as a Business

Step 3: Setting up your Instagram Business Profile

Step 4: Navigating through the app

Step 5: Posting images and videos on Instagram

Step 6: Finding Instagram Followers for your Business

Chapter V: The Top 10 Instagram Marketing Power Tools

You are using Instagram to empower your business with photos and videos.

It becomes a challenge for you to manage your Instagram marketing strategy on mobile. You can take advantage of some online tools that will allow you to do more with Instagram.

So, here are some tools that will help you build your Instagram followers and engagement with your audience. These tools also help you measure your success with Instagram.

Collecto:

Followgram has changed into Collecto. You can

extend your Instagram account's functionality with Collecto. Collecto allows you to have an elegant web interface that manages your presence on Instagram. The stats section synchronizes your data and provides you with an overview about your account activity. You can include RSS feed, follow button, WordPress widget and QR code to your public profile.

Collecto enhances your browsing features and provides geo based recommendations, so you can connect with your audience on Instagram and build your local communities. Collecto also provides paid plans to extend your reach on Instagram.

You can choose plans according to your business. For the pro plan you have to pay 19.00€ per/year and for the brand plan you need to pay 249.00€ per/year.

You can include custom background and custom cover photo on your public Instagram account. You can also send private messages to your followers.

Iconosquare:

Iconosquare is a user friendly web interface to manage your Instagram account which is also known as Statigram. You can include add-ons to your Instagram account.

The best thing about Iconosquare is its statistics features. It provides you the information on how you can optimize your Instagram account to get the most engagement. You can monitor your growth, check your account history monthly or weekly, and find most engaged followers with community insights.

Magnifying icon helps you find the followers who don't follow you back.

With Instagram feed tab, you can inform your other social media communities that you are on Instagram. You can interact with your followers by liking, commenting and sharing posts on social media. You can also set up image and video contests and promote them to increase your brand awareness and engagement. If you are searching for effective and scalable Instagram strategy, you should go for Iconosquare.

INK361:

Ink361 is a free web interface that allows you to view your Instagram feed on desktop means .Images will be displayed much bigger than mobile. Ink361 helps you to create custom albums and share those custom albums photos with non-Instagram users. You can allow your visitors to share your visuals on social media platform.

The unique feature of ink361 is that it allows you to redesign your real images and convert them into highly attractive and appreciable pieces of art. It ensures that your clicks will receive their due worth.

You can look for new friends and follow them based on your interests. You can organize your campaign by sorting people who are following you and set alert for new posts. Ink361 gives you a clear overview about your Instagram statistics and keeps track of your social media impact.

Chapter VI: The Hottest 10 Instagram Marketing Tips

Instagram can be used as a powerful tool for boosting the sales and customer engagement of your business.

It provides a gateway which, if properly followed, can channel your marketing efforts in the right direction. Instagram helps you to convert your simple photos into highly effective and usable snapshots.

A proper and authentic use of Instagram can ensure smooth and effective running of your business long term. Following our tips ensures that Instagram usage proves to be a fruitful exercise for your business:

Reward your followers- Always remember, the success or failure of any business depends on how well you take care of your loyal customers. These people have stood by you in the long run, so you need to devise suitable strategies to keep them engaged in the long run. Give them a sneak peek into your product before you make it available to general buyers.

Make them feel connected to your organization by taking their valuable feedback. Certain points like additional discounts and free shipping, etc. can make your customers turn into loyalists. Always ensure that they feel connected to your brand on a personal level.

Showcase your products like never before- Instagram enables you to present your products to your customers in an uncomplicated and dignified manner.

Certain exclusive features allow you to create extremely eye-pleasing images for your products that will lure your customers into purchasing.

The key to a successful product lies in the effective depiction of its features to the customer base. The characteristics of your product and its features can be easily highlighted with Instagram's help. Share the snapshots of your product and its features with your customers. And with Instagram, you surely are going in the right direction.

Highlight your product creation process- One of the basic doubts in the minds of the customer is how the product gets manufactured: what are the basic processes that your company puts into practice before the manufacturing process gets operational?

Do you follow the pre-defined industry standards or not? The answer to all these mind boggling queries is Instagram.

Create a sequential and step- by- step photo series that showcases the complete manufacturing process. Also, if you find that the process is quite complex, you can create more than one guide and show the different stages right from planning to production to delivery.

Chapter VII: Shocking Instagram Businesses' Case Studies

Here you will find business case studies with Instagram that will show you how businesses are increasing their brand awareness and revenue, how brands use their level of creativity to capture more audience's attention, and how they show their real customers examples to enhance their database.

Levi's:

Levi's is an iconic San Francisco denim clothing brand. Its jeans are the most known and emulated clothing in world. Levis has 359,729 followers on Instagram. Levis wanted to be at the forefront of customers' minds and increase its brand awareness among audiences.

Levis ran a 9 day campaign in November; they showcased four photos of their customers who were dressed with unique denim fabric and shared photos of memorable times in beautiful outdoor spaces. These photos ads were aimed at 18-34 aged audiences in U.S.

Results were awesome, as Levi's posts reached 7.4 million viewers who visit Instagram on a regular basis to get motivated by well-crafted images, and they saw a 24% lift in ad recall.

Director of digital Levis Julie Channing said, "Not only were we able to reach a large audience with our ads on Instagram, but the metrics clearly show we engaged with them in a memorable and authentic way. We're pleased with these results."

Chobani:

Chobani is founded by Hamdi Ulukaya in 2005, New York.

They are unique in creating their appetizing and nutritive yogurt that is prepared with natural ingredients. The goal of Chobani was to change the outlook of people towards yogurt being great for any meal rather than only for breakfast.

Chobani ran a four week campaign in which they targeted females aged 18-49 in U.S. They posted images of quick breakfasts, a savory snack and an indulgent dessert images that can be made with yogurt.

Chobani reached 4 million users in U.S., 22% lift in recall, 7% lift in people who used Chobani anytime in a day.

Julie Channing, Director of Digital told, "Instagram is a great platform for Chobani. It allows us to show how people actually use our product and inspires new ways to savor. This campaign showcased delicious creations and different times of day, extending our existing presence of real, beautiful imagery to new audiences and effectively changing people's perceptions about enjoying Chobani throughout the day."

Taco Bell:

Taco bell is a fast food restaurant, founded in 1962 and based in California. Taco bell has 473,964 million followers. Taco bell wanted to increase brand awareness about its new breakfast line launch among 18-44 aged people.

Taco bell created a campaign "Live Más" for four weeks and illustrated it in a unique manner, which was inspired by Instagram community to resonate with its targeted audience. Taco Bell's creative team delivered a series of pictures on Instagram; those pictures included fun and active lifestyle images of friends having breakfast, and each image captured their brand's youthfulness.

The response was awesome; Taco Bell reached a 12.5 million member audience of 18-44 year-olds in the U.S. in four weeks and saw 29% lift in ad recall that is 4X higher than control.

Chris Brandt, Chief Marketing Officer of Taco Bell said, "We let the concept drive creative production and paired that with what we knew about how people engage on Instagram. What resulted was a powerful visual narrative for our new breakfast menu that was a perfect fit within the Instagram environment."

Chapter VIII: Instagram Marketing Dos and Don'ts

Instagram has proved to be one of the most useful and vital tools for making your business effective.

Meticulous planning will be the key to success. A careful and planned approach will ensure that managing your business becomes a cakewalk.

The pros and cons will be present everywhere; it all depends on you how you tackle these issues.

Dos

Here you will find a list of certain important points that you should keep in mind while we use Instagram- Share your knowledge with others- Instagram provides you with a unique opportunity to share what you know with a huge customer base. It enables you make effective and efficient use of technology for creating brand awareness.

For example, Valeen Parubchenko, director of Private Picassos, a Company that provides art lessons in New York, uses this tool to monitor the projects of her students from the beginning till the end.

Introduce new products- Instagram is a great launch pad for your product or service. With the constant increase in the number of Instagram users, businesses have started using this as a marketing tool. By running advertising campaigns on Instagram, you can generate a huge number of leads, which gives you immense business potential.

Show customers who uses your product- It's always a great idea to show people who have been using your products of late. It gives them a feeling of belonging, and they feel connected to your brand. For example, Benefit Cosmetics used Instagram to find out how many people were using their products. It got a huge response and approximately 12,000 people submitted their images. Later on, as a return favor, it created a mosaic view and displayed it on its website.

Being precise is always beneficial-. Being precise means posting photos that are a mirror image of you and your product. Being informative and clear about your point is the focal point of any business activity. Be genuine to the customers if you want them to be with you. Let your images speak for themselves.

Connect with your customers- Instagram gives you an opportunity to develop a rapport with your client base. It helps you to have a look at their snaps and respond instantly. Remember, you should always mention them while replying.

For example, use #markinc when you want your comments to reach Mark directly.

Design a suitable advertising strategy- Instagram allows you to develop direct access with your customers. Make sure that a planned approach and careful policy is designed for your advertising. Never have an ambiguous strategy for your product. For example, Levi's was one of the first advertisers on Instagram that used its images to establish a direct connection with its customers.

Hold customer engaging contests- Running a contest is one of the best available ways in which you can engage your audience for your benefits. Offer them gifts, provide them with take-away and make them feel that you always have something interesting in store for them.

Focus on your product only- Instagram gives you a chance to show diverse uses for your product. However, you should always be product-centered. If you deviate a little away from your product, it can have negative results for your company.

Effective use of filters- Instagram presents a unique way to substantiate the quality of your photos. Making proper and effective use of these filters ensures that your clicks get converted into highly appreciable content. Also, keep in mind these filters have been created for your benefit, not for invading any other person's privacy.

Promote your hard work- If you have put your heart and soul into creating a certain product, show your customers that. Remember, they are the ones who use your product, and they will always be willing to hear details about the efforts you incur for their creation.

Don'ts

Here are some points that you should never implement if you want to have a successful journey with Instagram-Don't upload pictures of others- The basic reason for the creation of Instagram was to enable people to share their personal snapshots with their near and dear ones. Also you need to keep in mind that the beauty of Instagram lies in sharing the images that you clicked to share with your closed user group. So, let's avail the benefits and not play spoilsport in the life of others.

Don't like all the snapshots- Yes, it's true that you might have a large group of friends, but you cannot go on liking each and every snap. Learn to be selective, not because you want to reduce the social connection, but because selectivity is a quality of the learned.

Don't have time gap in your posts- One thing that adversely affects your brand and its growth scope is having a considerable time gap between your posts.

Try and maintain a certain level of connectivity in your posts so that your closed group remains in touch with you.

Don't make excessive use of hashtags- Hashtags can have a drastic impact on the effectiveness of your Instagram usage. Some of the most popular users of Instagram have made selective use of hashtags, which has enabled them to be recognized on a larger scale. Overuse of everything is bad.

Don't get negative- Understand the simple fact that if you upload a snap, it is liable to get appreciation as well as some grey feedback. Criticism should be welcomed with open arms. So, do not get overly cautious or overly curious.

People have opinions, and you cannot control their thought processes.

Don't deviate from your priorities-"Your time is finite, but your work area infinite". Instagram enables you to connect with your customer base instantly.

But, deviations are very dangerous for attaining targets. Being focused leads to the path of prosperity and success of your enterprise.

Don't restrict it only to advertising purposes- The utilities of Instagram should not be restricted to only promoting your brand. Focus on sharing the facts and features in a different way. This will appeal to people because they can become quite bored with the age-old marketing tools and techniques.

Don't forget to design your unique video- The relevance of getting sales conversions with the help of videos has been proven over and over again. It becomes quite easy to engage your audience this way. Go ahead, challenge yourself, create your video and keep marching on the path of success.

Don't post dis-respectful content- Instagram gives you an opportunity to get in touch with a huge bank of customers. Always keep in mind that you need to treat others the way you want to be treated. So, upload photos that do not invade in the privacy of others.

Don't forget to comment back- Yes, always keep in mind it's very important to give a personal touch to your customers. Depending on the size, it might be a little difficult for you to respond back to each and every one, but efforts need to be put in place. Try to make communication a two way process for engaging the audience

Conclusion:

We're thrilled that you have chosen to take advantage of our Special Free Report, and we wish you amazing success. And in order to take your Instagram Marketing even farther, we invite you to get the most out of Instagram by getting access to our complete Training System by clicking here Thanks so much for the time you have dedicated to learning how to get the most advantages from Instagram. Instagram has come to stay in the market forever.

About The Author

AUTHOR NAME is *ClydeX*

Find out more at digitalexplorerx.com

www.ingramcontent.com/pod-product-compliance
Lightning Source LLC
Chambersburg PA
CBHW050034230526
45470CB00003B/1273